Please, Puppy, Please

by Spike Lee & Tonya Lewis Lee

illustrations by Kadir Nelson

SCHOLASTIC INC.

New York Toronto London Auckland Sydney
Mexico City New Delhi Hong Kong Buenos Aires

For information regarding permission, write to Simon & Schuster Books for Young Readers, Simon & Schuster Children's Publishing Division, 1230 Avenue of the Americas, New York, NY 10020.

ISBN-13: 978-0-439-89564-4

ISBN-10: 0-439-89564-2

Published by Scholastic Inc., 557 Broadway, New York, NY 10012, by arrangement with Simon & Schuster Books for Young Readers, Simon & Schuster Children's Publishing Division.

12 11 10 9 8 7 6 5 4 3 2 1 6 7 8 9 10 11/0

Printed in the U.S.A. 08

First Scholastic printing, September 2006

Book design by Dan Potash

The text for this book is set in Imperfect Bold.

The illustrations for this book are rendered in oils.

For Satchel, Jackson, and Ginger . . .

you are all doing just fine!

—T. L. L. and S. L.

For Amel and Aya, my little jitterbugs. Love, Daddy.

—K. N.

Stay inside today,

puppy puppy, please, puppy.

Outside? Let's go play,
puppy, puppy, puppy, please.

Away from the gate,
puppy puppy,
please, puppy.

Oh wait, **puppy**, wait,
please, please, please,

please.

Come back here! Don't go,

puppy puppy, please, puppy.

Not the mud, puppy. Oh no,

puppy, puppy, puppy,

please.

Rub-a-dub-dub,
please, please,
puppy puppy?

Get back in the tub,

Puppy Puppy Puppy,

please!

Watch out for the cat,

puppy, please, puppy,

please!

Oh no, don't do that,

puppy puppy,

please, puppy!

Fetch me the ball,
puppy, puppy, puppy, **please!**

Come when I call,
puppy, please, please, please,
please!

You're doing just fine,
puppy puppy
puppy puppy.

Always be mine,
puppy, please, puppy, please.